God's Words for God's People

By Diana Stewart

God's Words for God's People

God's Word for God's People
© 2012 by Diana Stewart
Printed in the United States of America
Revised 2020
ISBN 978-0-9852094-2-1

All rights reserved solely by the author. The author guarantees all contents are original and do not infringe upon the legal rights of any other person or work. No part of this book may be reproduced in any form without the permission of the author.

The views expressed in this book are not necessarily those of the publisher.

Unless otherwise indicated, Bible quotations are taken from the New King James version of the Bible. Copyright © 1982 by Thomas Nelson.

Cover design by Mark Greenaway

.

www.trueperspectivepublishinghouse.com

AUTOGRAPH PAGE

Autograph this book as a personal investment to yourself or the life of someone that God has put in your path on this life journey.

_____

ACKNOWLEDGMENTS

I dedicate this book to the one who is the author and finisher of all things great and small, my Lord and Savior Jesus Christ, the one who is the head of my life. Thank you Lord for giving me the vision for this book.

I would like to thank my children Dave, Latonia and Paul Jr. for their patience and help during the process of me writing this book. I would like to give a special thanks to my spiritual advisors, my church family, my Pastor and all of my co-workers.

Table of Contents

The Way of Salvation.........................2

How to Commit your Life to Christ.........6

How to Receive Understanding..............10

How to Draw Near to God...................14

How to Have an Effective Prayer Life....18

How to Build Your Faith...................22

How to Give to God's Work.................26

What is the Importance of Obedience......30

How to Overcome Satan....................34

Strength in Time of Weakness.............38

Courage in Time of Fear..................44

Peace in the Time of Anxiety.............48

Guidance in Time of Decisions.............52

How to Survive Financial Problems......... 56

Relief in Time of Sickness...................60

Comfort in Time of Sorrow...................64

How to Control Your Tongue...............68

There is Power in the Blood 72

How to Wait on God.................................78

Sign of His Coming 82

INTRODUCTION

God's words in the bible are so powerful and He wrote them for us, His people. Sometimes when reading the bible we are easily overwhelmed with so many meaningful words and stories. This book captures key scriptures and categorizes them for easy reference and review.

Some of the categories include, When You Need Peace, Relief in Time of Sickness, How to Control Your Tongue, How to Have an Effective Prayer Life and How to Overcome Satan. I also explain how to put the scriptures into action in your life for your personal growth in the Lord.

God's Words for God's People

THE WAY OF SALVATION

Ye shall not need to fight in this battle. Set yourselves, stand ye still, and see the salvation of the Lord with you. O Judah and Jerusalem: fear not nor be dismayed: Tomorrow go out against them: for the Lord will be with you.
(2 Chronicles 20: 17)

For he saith, I have heard thee in a time accepted, and in the day of salvation have I succored thee: behold, now is the day of salvation. (2 Corinthians 6 :2)

Jesus answered and said unto him, verily, verily, I say unto thee, except a man be born again, he cannot see the Kingdom of God.
(John 3:3)

For God so loved the world that HE gave His only begotten Son, that whosoever believeth in Him should not perish but have everlasting life.
(John 3:16)

For I am not ashamed of the gospel of Christ: for it is the power of God unto salvation to everyone they believeth; to the Jew first, and also to the Greek. (Romans 1:16)

That if thou shall confess with thy mouth the Lord Jesus and shall believe in thine heart that God hath raised Him from the dead, thou shall be saved.
(Romans 10:9)

Lead me in thy truth and teach me; for thou art the God of My salvation; and on Thee do I wait all the day.
(Psalm 25:5)

Who are kept by the power of God through faith unto salvation ready to be revealed in the last time. (1 Peter 1:5)

Neither is there salvation in any other for there is none other name under heaven given among men, whereby we must be saved
(Acts 4:12

Who hath saved us, and called us with an holy calling, not according to our works, but according to his own purpose and grace, which was given us in Christ Jesus before the world began.
(1Timothy 1:9)

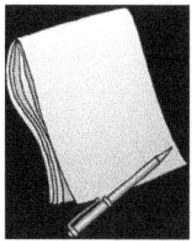

Note: *The Way to Salvation*

The way to salvation is simple and easy. People often make being saved look hard. Becoming saved is when you give your life to Christ and allow Him to be everything in your life. You must first confess with your mouth all of your wrongdoings and then turn away from those things.

It's a Belief in your mind, soul and heart that Jesus died on the cross for you and that on the third day He arose with all power in His hands and now sits at the right hand of God the Father almighty. After confession of your sins, you must find a church to attend so that you may grow in Him and allow God to work in you, through you and for you. He wants us to be humble and do His will until He comes.

In order for God to do things in us, for us and through us, we must be clean and holy. God made the world and the fullness therein. All it takes is a decision to receive Christ as your Savior. You must be serious and know that you are ready to grow up and lay aside foolish and sinful ways. If this is you, all you have to do is repeat this simple prayer and allow God to be the head of your life.

PRAYER:

Dear heavenly Father, I humbly come to you as a sinner. I want you to come into my life so that I may be saved. I believe in my heart that you died on the cross for my sins and were raised for my justification. I now turn away from my evil ways and now serve you. Come into my life dear Jesus and be the head of my life. I receive you now as my Lord and Savior in Jesus' name. AMEN

Now that you have decided to receive Christ, we encourage you to prayerfully seek a local church, congregation or assembly that will assist you in growing as a new Christian by the clear teaching of the Bible.
2 Peter 3:18

Read these Scriptures:

1. God loves you (John 3:16, Roman 5:8)
2. All are sinners (Romans 3:10, 23)
3. God's remedy for sin (Romans 6:23, John 1:12, 1 Corinthians 15: 3-4)
4. All may be saved now (Revelation 3:20, Romans 10:13)
5. Assurance as a Believer (Romans 10:9, John 5:24, John 20:31)

By Harriett Condry-Brayboy

HOW TO COMMIT YOUR LIFE TO CHRIST

Trust in the Lord, and do good; dwell in the land, and feed on His faithfulness. Delight yourself also in the Lord; And He shall give you the desires of your heart. Commit your way to the Lord, trust also in Him, and He shall bring it to pass. He shall bring forth your righteousness as the light, and your justice as the noonday. Rest in the Lord, and wait patiently for Him; do not fret because of him who prospers in his way, because of the man who brings wicked schemes to pass.
(Psalm 37:3-7)

Seek the Lord while He may be found, call upon Him while He is near. Let the wicked forsake his way, and the unrighteous man his thoughts; Let him return to the Lord, and He will have mercy on him; and to our God, for He will abundantly pardon.
(Isaiah 55:6-7)

Let your heart therefore be perfect with the Lord our God, to walk in his statues, and to keep his commandments, as at the day.
(1 Kings 8:61)

But without faith it is impossible to please Him, for he who comes to God must believe that He is, and that He is a rewarder of those who diligently seek Him.
  (Hebrews 11:6)

The Lord is not slack concerning His promise, as some count slackness, but is longsuffering toward us,[a] not willing that any should perish but that all should come to repentance. But grow in the grace and knowledge of our Lord and Savior Jesus Christ. To Him be the glory both now and forever. Amen.
(2 Peter 9:9, 18)

For God so loved the world, that he gave his only begotten Son, that whosoever believeth in him should not perish, but have everlasting life. (John 3:16)

Whosoever believeth that Jesus is the Christ is born of God: and everyone that loveth him that begat loveth him also that is begotten of him. For this is the love of God, that we keep his commandments: and his commandments are not grievous.
(1 John 5:2-3)

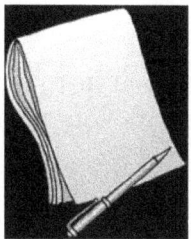

Note: How to Commit your Life to Christ

*W*hen you commit to something, you do it wholeheartedly. You do whatever you have to do to make sure you are putting forth great effort to succeed in that thing. Committing your life to God should have that same drive. You should do what is necessary to make sure you succeed at being a Kingdom Builder. He expects a work for the Kingdom out of you. He doesn't expect you to only perform your work, he expects you to make a commitment to work for his purpose alone. Sometimes we forgot who we are in Christ and forget our true purpose. As a child of God you should come to him daily for forgiveness of your sins. David made a commitment to God after asking God for forgiveness of his sin. He made a commitment to dwell in the house of God forever. A few years ago, I was so sick from the hands of my enemy, but I made a commitment to God. I told the Lord if he healed me I would serve him until I leave this world to be home with him in paradise (HEAVEN). My desire is to do great work in his kingdom and stay in fellowship with other believers. What does it mean to commit your life to Christ? Seek the Lord with all your heart daily.

Having a personal relationship with Christ is the most important decision you will ever make in your life.

Prayer

Heavenly father, I place myself in your presence Lord, I give you praise, I honor you and glorify your name because you are worthy to be praised.

I worship you as Creator and Ruler of heaven and earth. Now I make the commitment that I believe that your son Jesus Christ was crucified and died on the cross for my sins.

Jesus, out of your love for me you suffered your sorrowful passion. I now accept your unfailing love. Jesus with your help I will turn away from sin. I know you will wash and cleanse me from all my sins and lead me to the path of righteousness. In Jesus name I pray. Amen

HOW TO RECEIVE UNDERSTANDING

Forsake foolishness and live, and go in the way of understanding. "The fear of the Lord is the beginning of wisdom, and the knowledge of the Holy One is understanding.
(Proverbs 9:6, 10)

Understanding is a wellspring of life to him who has it. But the correction of fools is folly.
(Proverbs 16:22)

Counsel is mine, and sound wisdom; I am understanding, I have strength.
(Proverbs 8:14)

The fear of the Lord is the beginning of wisdom; A good understanding have all those who do His commandments. His praise endures forever.
(Psalm 111:10)

Thus saith the LORD, Let not the wise man glory in his wisdom, neither let the mighty man glory in his might, let not the rich man glory in his riches: But let him that glorieth glory in this, that he understandeth and knoweth me, that I am the LORD which exercise lovingkindness, judgment, and righteousness, in the earth: for in these things I delight, saith the LORD.
 (Jeremiah 9:23-24)

Get wisdom! Get understanding! Do not forget, nor turn away from the words of my mouth. Do not forsake her, and she will preserve you; love her, and she will keep you. Wisdom is the principal thing; therefore get wisdom. And in all your getting, get understanding.
(Proverbs 4:5-7)

But there is a spirit in man, and the breath of the Almighty gives him understanding.
(Job 32:8)

And to love him with all the heart, and with all the understanding, and with all the soul, and with all the strength, and to love his neighbor as himself, is more than all whole burnt offering and sacrifices.
(Mark 12:33)

Note: *How to Receive Understanding*

*W*e will never understand all that we experience in this life on our own. We have to trust God to give us understanding. Tell God your situation and he will direct you to the Word of God, which will allow you to gain understanding. The more knowledgeable you get in the Word, the more understanding you will obtain and subsequently the more wisdom you will have. The accuracy of God's word is everlasting and not an opinion. In order to have understanding we have to diligently seek God and he will in turn direct our path. The bible gives us many examples of right and wrong actions and that is why we have to trust in the Lord and lean not to our own understanding.

Dear Lord, we give you praise and glorify your name, because you are great. Lord, the trials and difficulties that we face every day seems at times to take up so much of our thoughts. Lord we ask that you give us a deeper understanding of how to pray and live in your perfect and eternal will, for you have put eternity in our heart and we desire to pray in your spirit and in line with your will. Lord give us understanding and knowledge every day. Give us a single vision of your will, a mind to focus on you and the courage to pray into your will in the power of the Holy Spirit and not in the flesh. Protect us from the strategies of the enemy who prowls around like a roaring lion seeking a prey to devour and dismantle by your holy spirit of power. We ask this in Jesus Precious name. Amen

HOW TO DRAW NEAR TO GOD

Seek the Lord and His strength; Seek His face evermore! Remember His marvelous works which He has done, His wonders, and the judgments of His mouth.
(1 Chronicles 16:11-12)

I love those who love me, and those who seek me diligently will find me.
(Proverbs 8:17)

As the deer pants for the water brooks, so pants my soul for You, O God. Deep calls unto deep at the noise of Your waterfalls; all Your waves and billows have gone over me. The Lord will command His loving kindness in the daytime, And in the night His song shall be with me— A prayer to the God of my life.
(Psalm 42:1; 7-8)

God's Words for God's People

I wait for the Lord, my soul waits, and in His word I do hope. My soul waits for the Lord more than those who watch for the morning— Yes, more than those who watch for the morning.
(Psalm 130:5-6)

My soul, wait silently for God alone, for my expectation is from Him.
(Psalm 62:5)

Hear my cry, O God; attend to my prayer. From the end of the earth I will cry to You when my heart is overwhelmed; lead me to the rock that is higher than I.
(Psalm 61: 1-2)

Draw near to God and He will draw near to you. Cleanse your hands, you sinners; and purify your hearts, you double-minded. 9 Lament and mourn and weep! Let your laughter be turned to mourning and your joy to gloom. 10 Humble yourselves in the sight of the Lord, and He will lift you up.
(James 4:8-10)

However, one that thirsteth, come ye to the waters, and he that hath no money: come ye, buy, and eat: yea, come, buy wine and milk without money and without price. Cline your ear and come unto me: and eat ye that which is good, and let your soul delight itself in fatness.
(Isaiah 55:1-3)

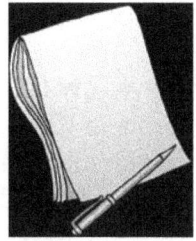

Note: *How to Draw Near to God*

After accepting Jesus as Savior, you have to get to a place of building that relationship. Building a Friendship with God is like that of building a friendship with someone only instead of being physical, it's spiritual. You have to talk to him often, share your life with him and allow him to speak back to you. How can you talk to God? I believe that God speak to us in many different ways, through prayer, the bible, worship etc. The lord always speak to me in my shower, when I am driving and when I am fasting. When we enter into the presence of the Lord, we will find security, and safety, and comfort, it doesn't matter how dark the world is around us, there is peace for the soul in the presence of our Savior. God wants to have a close relationship with you. His word says "If you draw close to Him, He will draw close to you! Why don't you talk to him today?

Prayer to Help You Draw Near to God

Dear God, take full control over my life today, Lord I acknowledge you as my Lord and King, my Savior, my Redeemer and my Healer. Keep me from sinning against you, today Lord. Help me to abide in you and make me a woman/man of your word and prayer, Help me to fix my eyes, not on what is seen, but also the things that are unseen, And if I should grow weary, discouraged, depressed or frustrated, help me I pray O Lord, to remember who you are, and to whom I belong. Lord show me where you brought me from, and where I could have been. Lord you are my hope, my peace, my Comforter and my Deliver. Grant me a breakthrough today and draw me closer to you, so I can fulfill my purpose and do your will. Keep my eyes from tears and my feet from falling. Bless my home, bless my loved ones, family and friends, and bless the labor of my hands I pray. In Jesus mighty name I pray.
 Amen

HOW TO HAVE AN EFFECTIVE PRAYER LIFE

Let us therefore come boldly to the throne of grace; that we may obtain mercy and find grace to help in time of need.
(Hebrews 4:16)

"And when you pray, you shall not be like the hypocrites. For they love to pray standing in the synagogues and on the corners of the streets, that they may be seen by men. Assuredly, I say to you, they have their reward. 6 But you, when you pray, go into your room, and when you have shut your door, pray to your Father who is in the secret place; and your Father who sees in secret will reward you openly."
(Matthew 6: 5-6)

Evening and morning and at noon I will pray, and cry aloud, and He shall hear my voice.
(Psalm 55:17)

Therefore, I say unto you what thing soever ye desire, when ye pray, believe that ye receive them, and ye shall have them. And when ye stand praying, forever, if ye ought against any: that your Father also which is in heaven may forgive you your trespasses. (Mark 11:24-25)

Wisdom is the principal thing: therefore get wisdom: and with all thy getting get understanding. (proverbs 4:7)

Let us come before him with thanksgiving and extol him with

Music and song.
   (Psalm 95:2)

   In the morning, LORD, you hear my voice; in the morning I lay my requests before you and wait expectantly.
   (Psalm 5:3)

   You will make your prayer to Him, He will hear you, and you will pay your vows. You will also declare a thing, and it will be established for you; So light will shine on your ways.
   (Job 22:27-28)

Lord, I cry out to You make haste to me! Give ear to my voice

when I cry out to You. Let my prayer be set before You as incense, The lifting up of my hands as the evening sacrifice.
   (Psalm 141:1-2)

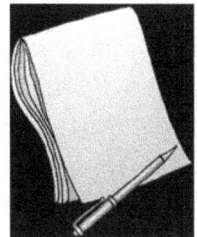

Note: How to have an Effective Prayer Life

  Read your bible and pray daily. In everything you do, seek God first. God repeatedly calls upon His children to come to Him when we have problems or difficulties in our lives. We must first go to Him when we recognize our sinfulness and call upon Him for mercy to forgive us of our sins and impart in us His Holy Spirit to direct us.

  Our daily prayers should include help for making choices and/or decisions, for forgiveness of our sins, deliverance from our evil ways, and to petition Him for protection and provision. The more you pray the more the Holy Spirit will impart on you a willing spirit to live a Godly life. And in doing so, you will be able to conquer the fight with your flesh.

Our relationship with God soars to a much higher depth as we enter into a daily communion with Him. I encourage you to renew or begin your prayer life with Him today. Take some time during your prayer to also listen for His thoughts and plans for you. The power of prayer is in you, who prays it and in God, who hears it.

Prayer makes a difference and can be life changing. David prayed scriptures and if you haven't mastered praying as yet, pray those familiar scriptures that you know. Also, search the bible for those problems or circumstances that you may have to see what God has to say concerning them. I would highly encourage you to pray those scriptures and ask God to manifest Himself in those situations and turn them around.

HOW TO BUILD YOUR FAITH

For in the righteousness of God is revealed from faith to faith; as it is written, "The just shall live by faith."
(Romans 1:17)

Whom have I in heaven but You? And there is none upon earth that I desire beside You. My flesh and heart may fail; but God is the strength of my heart and my portion forever.
(Psalm 73: 25-26)

Wherefore if God so clothe the grass of the filed, which today is and tomorrow is cast into the oven, shall He not much more clothe you, O ye of little faith?
(Matthew 6: 30)

When Jesus heard it, He marveled and said to them that followed, "Verily I say unto you, I have not found so great faith, no not in Israel."
(Matthew 8: 10)

Jesus answered and said unto them, "Verily I say unto you if ye have faith and doubt not, ye shall not only do this which is done to the fig tree but also if ye shall say unto this mountain, be thou removed and be thou cast into the sea; it shall be done."
(Matthew 21: 21)

And Peter calling to remembrance said unto Him, Master behold the fig tree which thou cursedst is withered away. And Jesus answering saith unto them. Have faith in God.
(Mark 11: 21- 22)

And He said to the woman, "Thy faith hath saved thee, go in peace."
(Luke 7:50)

And the apostles said unto the Lord, increase our faith. And the Lord said, if ye had faith as a grain of mustard seed, ye might say unto this sycamine tree. Be thou plucked up by the root, and be thou planted in the sea: and it should obey you.
(Luke 17:5 -6)

And when they were come and gathered the church together, they rehearsed all that God had done with them and how He had opened the door of faith unto the Gentiles.
(Act 14: 27)

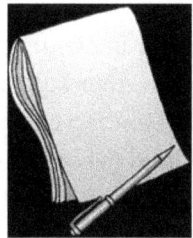

Note: How to Build your Faith

Building your faith can be challenging but doable. Faith comes by hearing and hearing by the word of God. To build your faith first you must not worry. If you worry then there's no need to pray. Worrying is the opposite of faith. I know it's difficult at times, but if you would put your heart and mind to it, pray and leave it in God's hands.

Once you place the problem, issue or circumstance in the hands of the Lord, at all cost, do not, pick it back up because you feel like He's taking too long. Have some patience! The word of God says that if we have faith the size of a grain of mustard seed, we can move mountains and mole hills.

Prayer is a key factor in building your faith as well. When you pray ask God to increase your faith and help you not to worry about your situation. Seek Him fervently and ask Him to give you that mustard seed faith. Go to the store and examine a package of mustard seed just see how much faith it takes to move God. Also, read and recite scriptures on faith this will help you in times of doubt and worry.

Prayer To Help You Build Your Faith in God

Father in Heaven, I give thanks to you this day; I give you honor, and I give you praise. I love you and adore you Lord because you are good. You are my strength and my defense when my heart is afraid. Give me a heart that will trust you.

Lord you are with me every step of the way and yet I sometimes lose faith, because of the fear of the outcome of my future. Faith cast out fear, while fear cast out faith. Lord help me to realize that only you know what the future holds and help me to trust you whenever I have doubts. Lord I know that your way is always the best way for me. Take hold of every decision concerning my life right now I pray in Jesus name.

Amen.

HOW TO GIVE TO GOD'S WORK

As soon as the commandment was circulated, the children of Israel brought in abundance the first fruits of grain and wine, oil and honey and of all the produce of the field; and they brought in abundantly the tithe of everything.
(2Chronicles 31:5)

He who has a generous eye will be blessed, For he gives of his bread to the poor.
(Proverbs 22:9)

He that giveth unto the poor shall not lack: but he that hideth his eyes shall have many a curse.(proverbs 28:27)

Cast your bread upon the waters, for you will find it after many days.
(Ecclesiastes 11:1)

'Take from among you an offering to the Lord. Whoever is of a willing heart, let him bring it as an offering to the Lord: gold, silver, and bronze;
(Exodus 35:5)

The righteous considers the cause of the poor, but the wicked does not understand such knowledge.
(Proverbs 29: 7)

"Do not lay up for yourselves treasures on earth, where moth and rust destroy and where thieves break in and steal; but lay up for yourself treasures in heaven, where neither moth nor rust destroys and where thieves do not break in and steal. For where your treasure is, there your heart will be also.
(Matthew 6:19-21)

Go ye therefore, and teach all nations, baptizing them in the name of the Father, and of the Son, and of the Holy Ghost: Teaching them to observe all things whatsoever I have commanded you: lo I am with you always, even unto the end of the world. A.-men
(Matthew 28:19-20)

Give to the Lord the glory due His name; bring an offering, and come into His courts.
(Psalm 96:8)

Note: How to Give to God's Work

The Bible says that there are some teachers, pastors, evangelists, etc., whatever your calling is, use it to Glorify God. If you can't give monetarily, give of your time in some area to assist in Kingdom building. Jesus called many people when he walked this earth. And now that his earthly ministry is over, Jesus calls us to work hard to spread the word and finish the mission he began. We all have responsibilities, according to our abilities. Some have heavier duties, some lighter. You have to work while it is day because when night comes, no man shall work. This means that there will come a time when Jesus returns and working to build the kingdom won't be needed; therefore you have to work while you are able to assist in building the God's Kingdom NOW!

Let Us Pray

Almighty God and everlasting father, we give you thanks for your saving grace and tender mercies toward us. We thank you for blessing us with another day, though it was not promised to us. We thank you for being our bountiful provider and for the many gifts that we enjoy so freely from the fruit of the earth. Help us to be wise servants and faithful stewards with the many blessing that we have received from your hands and may we take of what you give to us with grateful hearts and cheerfully give back to you a portion of your grace that we have received at your hand. Keep our hearts ever thankful towards you and give us your tender compassion for those around us that are hurting or in need. Lord give us a heart like yours. Help us to be willing to share our portion with others and may we show forth the love of God in our lives with a cheerful and graceful disposition especially for those who are needy. Lord I pray that our prayer will be accept, as we continue to give you glory and praise in Jesus name we pray.
    Amen.

WHAT IS THE IMPORTANCE OF OBEDIENCE?

But be doers of the word, and not hearers only, deceiving yourselves.
(James 1:22)

Casting down arguments and every high thing that exalts itself against the knowledge of God, bringing every thought into captivity to the obedience of Christ.
(2 Corinthians 10:5)

Whoever has no rule over his own spirit is like a city broken down, without walls.
(Proverbs 25:28)

And the world passeth away, and the lust therefore: but he that doeth the will of God abideth for ever. (1 John 2 :17)

For as by one man's disobedience many were made sinners. So by the obedience of one shall many be made righteous.(Romans 5:19)

Obey them that have the rule over you, and submit yourselves: for they watch for your souls, as they that must give account, that they may do it with joy, and not with grief: for that is unprofitable for you. (Hebrews 13:17)

And rend your heart, and not your garments; Return to the Lord your God, For He is gracious and merciful, Slow to anger, and of great kindness; And He relents from doing harm.
(Joel 2:13)

If you forsake the Lord and serve foreign gods, then He will turn and do you harm and consume you, after He has done you good." (Joshua 24:20)

If you are willing and obedient, you shall eat the good of the land; But if you refuse and rebel, You shall be devoured by the sword"; for the mouth of the Lord has spoken.
(Isaiah 1:19-20)

Now the just shall live by faith; but if anyone draws back, my soul has no pleasure in him."
(Hebrews 10:38)

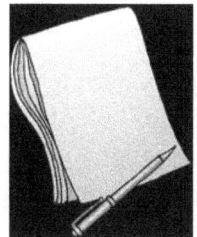

Note: *What is the importance of obedience?*

The bible says that Obedience is better than sacrifice. Obedience is very important in pleasing God. Obedience is the greatest worship that we can offer to God because when we obey, it deepens our relationship with Him. The word says, "Children obey your parents for this is right in the Lord". We must also obey the laws of the land, for this too is right in the Lord.

Obedience plays a vital role in everyday life; it is an expectation for people to obey authority, for example in the homes; parents expect obedience from their children. In school students are expected to obey their teachers, same expected in religions, and workplace. According to God holy words, we should obey our spiritual leaders and submit to them because they are keeping watch over our soul.

We obey God because we love him. There are faith, hope and love, and the greatest of these is love. But greater than love is obedience, if the love does not include obedience. Genuine love for God works out in stick obedience to God. Apart from obedience to the father there is no love for God and there is no kingdom of God. I have a passion to do the perfect will of God. I hope I never lose it. I count it as a great gift, one to be highly desire   and sought after. By his grace we are save.

Let us Pray

Father God, we thank you for another day; we thank you for your grace and your tender mercies. We thank you Lord, for loving us, for protecting us, and for giving us one more chance. You are a God of second chances. You are our Hope, our Rescue, our Deliverer, our Savior and our Redeemer. As the word says," God does not retain His anger forever; because he delights in steadfast love. 'Lord, we know your love knows no limits, nor your unfailing mercy possesses no boundaries; And so today Lord, we ask your forgiveness from all sins; known and unknown. Heal us internally and externally Lord and take complete control over us. Help us to know and trust you more; and to be obedient to your will and your way. Lord guide and direct us, individually and collectively, and cover us under your wings of protection. Help us, O God to be obedient children and also help us also to cast out of our heart and mind all things that might hinder us in a whole to love and forgive others who hurts us. As thou didst love the world, help us to love, as thou didst give thyself for us, help us to give ourselves to you. Help us to be humble and obedient servants and help us to reflect the love of Jesus Christ in our walk. We ask this in Jesus name. Amen.

HOW TO OVERCOME SATAN

But He turned and said unto Peter, Get thee behind Me satan: thou art an offense unto me; for thou savourest not the things that be of God, but those that be of men.
(Matthew 16: 23)

But Peter said Ananias why hath Satan filled thine heart to lie to the Holy Ghost, and to keep back part of the price of the land? (Acts 5:3)

To open their eyes and to turn them from darkness to light and from the power of Satan unto God that they may receive forgiveness of sins, and inheritance among them which are sanctified by faith that is in me.
(Acts 26:18)

Behold, I give unto you power to tread on serpents and scorpion, and over all the power by any means hurt you.
(Luke 10:19)

Submit yourselves therefore to God. Resist the devil and he will flee from you. Draw nigh to God, and He will draw nigh to you. Clean ye your hands, ye sinners: and purify your hearts, ye double minded.
(James 4: 7-8)

The Lord shall preserve thee from all evil: He shall preserve thy soul. The Lord shall preserve thy going out and thy coming in from this time forth and even for ever more.
(Psalm 121: 7-8)

Surely He shall deliver thee from the snare of the fowler, and from the noisome pestilence. A thousand shall fall at thy side and ten thousand at thy right hand: but it shall not come nigh thee.
(Psalm 91: 7-8)

To him that overcometh will I grant to sit with Me in my throne, even as I also overcame, and am set down with my father in His throne.
(Revelation 3: 21)

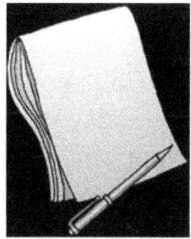

Note: How to Overcome Satan

Our only hope against Satan is Jesus Christ. Christ alone is more powerful than Satan. His grace brought us the Holy Spirit. Satan's job is to kill, steal and destroy. Guard yourself against Satan by keeping your eyes fixed on Jesus. Why do you think it is strange that we suffer persecution? Jesus said that this would happen, but we have to understand that Satan cannot do anymore to you than you allow him to. Be strong and courageous in the Lord. Putting on Christ's righteousness, stand firm in your identity in Christ. God provides powerful tools and strategies that we can use to stand against Satan. The most powerful tool is to renew our minds with the word of God. Romans 12:2 says "And be not conformed to this world: but be ye transformed by the renewing of your mind, that ye may prove what is that good and acceptable and perfect, will of God." There was a time in my life when I was straying away from the will of God all I was doing was trying to fit in with worldly activities, it opened up my door for the devil to enter my life, and attack my health. I had to regain my identify and know who I am in Christ and renew my mind back with the word of God so the devil could flee away from me. There is power in his word and there is power in the blood.

Let Us Pray

Great and mighty you are O God. You are our savior, Our Strength, and our Deliverer. Today we claim victory over Satan by putting on the whole armor of God. Lord help us to stand firm in the truth of your word so that we will not be victims of Satan's lies. Help us to guard our hearts from all evil so we can remain pure and holy, protected under the blood of Jesus Christ. Let no weapon that is formed against me and my family prosper. Lord, you said we should not be afraid of sudden terror, nor of trouble from the wicked when it comes, because you will give us confidence, Lord, we want to thank you for the spirit of faith, and not of fear; but of power, love and of a sound mind. You are our God who sits high and looks low; the only one who is able to see and do all things; and so today Lord, we ask that you dispatch your angels of mercy and protection around us. Let no evil befall us, nor any danger come upon us. Remove from our path and our lives O Lord, those who seek to deceive and destroy us. Cover our children and grandchildren Lord Jesus and keep them courageous and strong and in good health, lead and direct their paths. Give us a spirit of wisdom, compassion, patience and humility. Lord, we are prepared to live this day in spiritual victory, In Jesus name we pray. Amen.

STRENGHT IN TIME OF WEAKNESS

The Lord is my strength and song, and He is become my salvation: He is my God and I will prepare Him a habitation; my father's God, and I will exalt him.
(Exodus 15:2)

The Lord is my light and my salvation; whom shall I fear? The Lord is the strength of my life; of whom shall I be afraid?
(Psalm 27: 1)

The Lord is my strength and my shield: my heart trusted in Him. And I am helped: therefore my heart greatly rejoiceth: and with my song will I praise Him.
(Psalm 28: 7)

God is our refuge and strength, a very present help in trouble.
(Psalm 46: 1)

Honor and majesty are before Him: strength and beauty are in His sanctuary.
(Psalm 96:6)

The Lord is my strength and song, and is become my salvation.
(Psalm 118: 14)

He giveth power to the faint and to them that have no might he increaseth strength.
(Isaiah 40:29)

God is my strength and power and He maketh my way perfect.
(2 Samuel 22:33)

Watch and pray that ye enter not into temptation: the spirit indeed is willing but the flesh is weak.
(Matthew 26:41)

But God hath chosen the foolish things of the world to confound the wise: and God hath chosen the weak things of the world to confound the things which are mighty.
(1 Corinthian 1: 27)

Therefore I take pleasure in infirmities, in reproaches, in necessities, in reproaches, in persecutions, in distress. For Christ's sake: for when I am weak then I am strong.
(2 Corinthians 12:10)

He giveth power to the faint and to them that have no might He increaseth strength.
(Isaiah 40: 29)

Send thee help from the sanctuary and strength thee out of Zion.
(Psalm 20: 2)

That He would grant you, according to the riches of His glory, to be strength with might by His spirit in the inner man.
(Ephesians 3 16)

I can do all things through Christ who strengthens me.
(Philippians 4:13)

Strengthened with all might according to His glorious power, unto all patience and long suffering with joyfulness.
(Colossians 1: 11)

Prayer for Strength

Our Father who art in Heaven. I give you thanks for life and for your word; which is a lamp unto my feet, and a light unto my path. I come to you today feeling so weak and helpless there are many things on my mind, so many worries, so many trial and tribulation. Every time I think about what lies ahead of me, I feel overwhelmed. You said to come to you with our burdens and you will sustain us. The Bible says you are our Rock' 'and our'Fortress.'' you are all knowing and all powerful. You know the burden that I bear, and you allowed them to happen for a reason. Lord I may not see the purpose of them now, but I know that I can trust you, because you are an unfailing God, and you know what is best for me. Help me to be strong and remove the sprit weakness from me. In Jesus name. Amen.

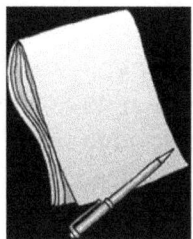

Note: *Strength in Time of Weakness*

Lord, when we are weak, you are strong; hold us in the palm of your hand. When you are feeling weak, go to God in prayer. God will strengthen you in your time of weakness. We are not our own. We belong to Him.

In everything you do, seek the Kingdom of God and His righteousness. The devil likes to show up in your time and areas of weaknesses. Be careful about what and who you entertain during this time. Whatever your weaknesses are, submit them to God and fast and pray about them. Once again, He is our strength in times when we are weak. God is love; He loves you and will never leave you nor forsake you.

During my time in college, I felt like giving up because I was going through a storm in my life, but with the strength and love of God and the support of my children, family and friends I kept going. God gave me the strength to endure and keep moving. Strength is about pushing through when everything inside you says quit. I was weak and burdened down by my situation, but God kept me, and he gave me the strength to fight to the end. Strength isn't about quitting, it's about the power of God that rises up on the inside of me that did not allow me to quit college. Strength is fighting when you want to give up on life, but with the love of God I rose up and pressed my way through.
God said "do not fear for I am with you; do not be dismayed, for I am your God. I will strengthen you and help you: I will uphold you with my righteous right hand." (Isaiah 41:10)

COURAGE IN TIME OF FEAR

Yea, though I walk through the valley of the shadow of death, I will fear no evil: For thou art with me: thy rod and they staff they comfort me.
(Psalm 23:4)

The Lord is my light and my salvation: Whom shall I fear? The Lord is the strength of my life: of whom shall I be afraid?
(Psalm 27:1)

O Fear the Lord, ye His saints for there is no want to them that fear Him.
(Psalm 34:9)

Let your conversation be without covetousness: be without covetousness: and be content with such things as ye have: For He hath said, I will never leave thee nor forsake thee.
(Hebrews 13: 5-6)

Be not afraid of sudden fear neither of desolation of the wicked, when it cometh.
(Proverbs 3:25)

God is our refuge and strength, a very present help in trouble. Therefore will not fear, though the earth be removed, and through the mountains be carried into the midst of the sea.
(Psalm 4: 1-2)

The fear of the Lord prolongeth days: but the years of the wicked shall be shortened.
(Proverb 10: 27)

Hear my cry, O God: attend unto my prayer. From the end of the earth will I cry unto thee, when my heart is overwhelmed: lead me to the rock that is higher than I.
(Psalm 61: 1-2)

Hear my voice, O God in my prayer: preserve my life from the fear of the enemy.
(Psalm 64:1)

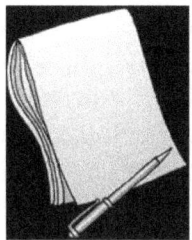

Note: *Courage in Time of Fear*

I remember when I was sick and full of fear. I had strayed from God and his covering and satan had deceived me and this put a lot of fear in me. I was so fearful that I was even afraid to return home from work at times. During this time, I was working at a Christian Private School and the teachers would pray and intercede on my behalf as well as encourage me.

Even though they prayed with and encouraged me, I was never released from my fears until I got closer to God. I started reading my bible daily, praying and attending church more often. It doesn't matter what you are going through, if you give it to God and allow Him to see you through, you can and will make it. Stay close to friends and family who are faithful in their walk with Christ and who are knowledgeable in the word so they can encourage you to move forward without being fearful.

Let Us Pray

What a friend we have in Jesus, all our sins and grieves to bear what a privilege to carry everything to my God in prayer. You tell us, I am the light of the world, Whoever follows me will never walk in darkness, but will have the light of life' 'Lord, send out your light and your truth today; let it lead, guide and direct us, so we may not stumble nor fall, or walk in the way of unrighteousness. Give us a heart of understanding, and bless us with your wisdom. Arise today O Lord, and release upon us your grace; redeem and restore us. Bring healing to those who are sick; deliver those who are in bondage; redirect the lost, give hope to the hopeless, strength the weary ones, and give peace to those whose hearts are hurting. Lord, keep us safe, keep us humble; guide and teach us how to walk in your goodness, righteousness and truth; and use us according to your will and purpose. Lord, we pray for your guidance, protection, deliverance and blessing upon our family, friends and loved ones. Draw them nearer to you O Lord and teach them your will and your way. Lord we honor you and give you thanks in Jesus name we pray. Amen.

PEACE IN THE TIME OF ANXIETY

Hear me when I call O God of my righteousness thou has enlarged me when I was in distress: have mercy upon me and hear my prayer.
(Psalm 4:1)

Be careful for nothing: but in everything by prayer and supplication with thanksgiving let your request be made known unto God. And the peace of God, which passeth all understanding, shall keep your hearts and minds through Christ Jesus.
(Philippians 4:6-7)

Let not your heart be troubled: ye believe in God. Believe also in me.
(John 14: 1)

Follow peace with all men, and holiness, without which no man shall see the Lord: (Hebrews 12:14)

O that thou hast hearkened to my commandments: then had thy peace been as a river and thy righteousness as the waves of the sea. (Isaiah 48: 18)

Glory to God in the highest, and on earth peace, goodwill toward me. (Luke 2: 14)

These things I have spoken unto you, that in me ye might have peace, in the world ye shall have tribulation: but be of good cheer: I have overcome the world.
(John 16:33)
Therefore being justified by faith, we have peace with God, through our Lord Jesus Christ. (Romans 5:1)

For He is our peace, who hath made both one, and hath broken down the middle wall of partition between us:
(Ephesians 2: 14)

A time to love, a time to hate: a time of war, and a time of peace. (Ecclesiastes 3:8)

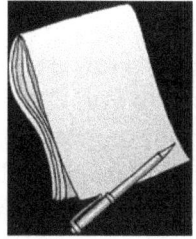

Note: *Peace in the Time of Anxiety*

I remember a time during my friend Harriett's life she didn't have peace with God. She was going through a terrible divorce, which lead to her anxiety. During that time whenever we conversed, she explained how the spirit of anxiety would attack her. She said, "that she would be driving and would sometimes feel like she was having an asthma attack, or she would be home and she would hear noises that would overwhelm her with so much fear because of the unknown. Harriett was really going through a hard time with the events going on in her life. It wasn't until she made up in her mind that she had to serve God whole-heartedly and subsequently renewed her faith in Christ that she discovered that peace that surpasses all understanding.

Don't allow the enemy to attack your mind, your spirit or your heart. Fear and anxiety are not of God. God is a God of peace. Keep your mind on God by reading and meditating on His word daily that you may hide it in your heart.

God's Words for God's People

Let Us Pray

Our father who art in heaven. How excellent is your name, and all honor and glory belongs to you. Lord, we come before your throne of grace, seeking your mercy. Your people are hurting Lord; we are faced with circumstances that we cannot tunnel through; so many challenges and situations that seems impossible. Lord, sometimes we lean on our own understanding, or turn to other places for help, forgetting that we can press in towards you, our Savior and our God, who never change, The God of all ages, who have the power to heal, deliver and set free. A Miracle working, all powerful, compassionate, kind, loving and forgiving God, who knows all our wounds and all our burdens we are carrying. Lord, we confess our need for you today. We place our hands into your hands Lord, as we seek your peace, healing and your grace. Restore hope in us Lord and strengthen us. Speak into the heart of your people and remind them of your word which tells us. 'Cast our cares upon you, Lord, speak to those who are about to give up. Let them know that you are the God in the good times and you are the God in the bad times, when things goes wrong in our life only you can make them right. Thank you for the privilege you gave us, so we can release to you all our needs, all our troubles, all our burdens and our concern to you. In Jesus name we pray. Amen

GUIDANCE IN THE TIME OF DECISIONS

And the Lord directs your heart into the love of God, and into the patient waiting for Christ.
(2 Thessalonians 3:5)

To give light to them that sit in darkness and in the shadow of death, guide our feet into the way of peace.
(Luke 1:79)

Howbeit when He, the Spirit of truth, is come, He will guide you into the truth: For He shall not speak of Himself: but whatsoever He shall hear, that He shall speak and He will show you things to come.
(John 16:13)

My voice shall though hear in the morning, O Lord, in the morning will I direct my prayer unto thee, and I will look up.
(Psalm 5:3)

Trust in the Lord with all thine heart: and lean not unto thine own understanding. In all thy ways acknowledge Him, and He shall direct thy path.
(Proverbs 3: 5-6)

A man's heart deviseth His way: but the Lord directeth his steps.
(Proverbs 16: 9)

If any of you lack wisdom, let him ask of God that giveth to all men liberally, and up braideth not; and it shall be given him. But let him ask in faith nothing wavering. For he that wavereth is like a wave of the sea driven with the wind and tossed.
(James 1: 5-6)

Let us therefore come boldly unto the throne of grace, that we may obtain mercy and find grace in time of need.
(Hebrews 4:16)

Note: *Guidance in Time of Decisions*

The Bible tells us, "In all thy ways acknowledge Him and He shall direct our paths." It is very important to seek the Lord for guidance when decisions are at hand. It doesn't matter how big or small the decision is, you have to seek the Lord. Constant prayer and fasting during this time will surely allow you to hear from the Lord and He will make it known what direction you should go concerning the decision that needs to be made
When I have a decision to make, my mind is consumed with it. I vacillate back and forth between the options. Its' all I can think about. I get anxious, I start to worry, and mull about it. I lie awake at night unable to sleep. I consider all the potential consequences to the choices, I just want a clear answer, because I don't want to make the wrong choice. For Example, leaving my home was a tough decision for me, but through fasting and praying God gave me the strength to make the right decision. When making a tough decision, it's important to search the scripture that can speak to our situation.

Let Us Pray

Bless the Lord, oh my soul, and all that is within me, bless his holy name. Father, I pray for peace upon my heart today, the peace of mind that will last eternally, a peace that only you can provide Lord, strengthen me and give me victory, Lord, from the enemy that brings confusion and worry into our minds. Oh Lord, fill me with your peace that will stand as the conviction in any decision I make in life. I thank you for your sprit that dwells within me, to guide and direct me into the path of peace. Your word tells us Lord, "For lack of guidance a nation falls but victory is won through many advisers." You say Lord, 'I will instruct you and teach you in the way you should go; I will counsel you with my loving eye on you' 'Lord I seek your face; I place my hands in your hands, and I place my trust in you; show me your path, so I may not lean on my own understanding. Lord give me a new start today and help me to persevere through whatever challenges that may confront me. Bless my life, bless my family, friends and loved ones; keep us safe and strong, and provide a way out for us, where there seems to be no way. Lord I honor you and give you the glory and I thank you for hearing the prayers I pray, In Jesus name. Amen.

HOW TO SURVIVE FINANCIAL PROBLEMS

Not that I speak in respect of want: for I have learned, in whatsoever state I am, therewith to be content. I know both how to be abased, and I know how to abound: everywhere and in all things I am instructed both to be full and to be hungry, both to abound and to suffer need. I can do all things through Christ which strengthened me.
(Philippians 4:11-13)

For the love of money is the root of all evil: which while some coveted after, they have erred from the faith, and pierced themselves through with many sorrows. But thou, O man of God, flee these things; and follow after righteousness, godliness, faith, love, patience, meekness.
(1 Timothy 6:10-11)

Trust in the Lord, and do good; so shalt thou dwell in the land, and verily thou shalt be fed. Delight thyself also in the Lord: and he shall give thee the desires of thine heart.
(Psalm 37:3-4)

I have been young, and now am old; yet have I not seen the righteous forsaken, nor his seed begging bread. He is ever merciful, and lendeth; and his seed is blessed.
(Psalm 37: 25-26)

But my God shall supply all your need according to his riches in glory by Christ Jesus.
(Philippians 4:19)

For you have need of patience, that after ye have done the will of God, ye might receive the promise.
(Hebrews 10:36)

He who trusteth in his riches shall fall: but the righteous shall flourish as a branch.
(Proverbs 11:28)

Remove far from me vanity and lies: give me neither poverty nor riches; feed me with food convenient for me.
(Proverbs 30:8)

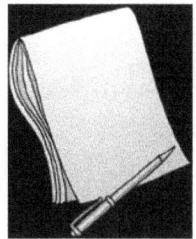

Note: *How to Survive Financial Problems*

Separating wants from needs is one essential part in surviving our financial woes. We must put God first in everything we do. A total commitment to God is the very first step to financial blessings. There are many Christians who still have not gained the victory in their finances due to principles in God's word that have been ignored. Are we giving God first, before paying others bills? (Proverbs 3:9-10) Honor the Lord with your wealth, with the first fruits off all your crops then your barns will be filled to overflowing, and your vats will brim over new wine. The Bibles tells us "to bring our tithes and offering to the storehouse." We have to be diligent in paying our tithes and offering and God will be diligent in supplying our needs. If we are faithful to Him; He will be faithful to us.

Let Us   Pray

We lift our eyes, and our heart to you O Lord, for you are our Creator, our Savior, and our keeper, Deliverer, our Redeemer, Strength, our Helper and our God. Lord, we surrender our financial affairs and concern about money to your Divine care and love. We ask that you remove our worries, anxieties and fears about our finances and replace them with faith. Lord, help us to manage our finances wisely and be faithful to your work and give to those in need. Help us to understand our purpose in life and to act on that purpose with courage and strength. Lord, help us to understand your heart for us, to breath, live and love in your freedom. Great is your faithfulness toward us; morning by morning, new mercies you have granted unto us. Keep us strong and courageous; give us wisdom and understanding; lead guide and direct us in everything we do and the plans we make. Let your grace and your mercy be upon us and give us victory in Jesus name we pray. Amen.

RELIEF IN TIME OF SICKNESS

O Lord rebuke me not in thy wrath: neither chasten me in thy hot displeasure.
(Psalm 38:1)

Forsake me not, O Lord O my God. Be not far from me. Make haste to keep me, O Lord my Salvation.
(Psalm 38: 21-22)

Is any sick among you? Let him call for the elders of the church: and let them pray over him, anointing him with oil in the name of the Lord and prayer of faith shall save the sick. And the Lord shall raise him up: and if he has committed sins, they be forgiven him. (James 5:14-15)

Behold, I will bring it health and cure, and I will cure them, and will reveal unto them the abundance of peace and truth.
(Jeremiah 33:6)

For I am persuaded that neither death not life not angels nor principalities, nor powers, nor things present, nor things to come, nor the height nor the depth, nor any creature, shall be able to separate us from the love of God, which is Christ Jesus our Lord.
(Romans 8: 38-39)

That it might be fulfilled which was spoken by Esaias the prophet saying, Himself took our infirmities and bore our sickness.
(Matthew 8: 17)

The Lord will strengthen him upon the bed of languishing. Thou wilt make all his bed in his sickness.
(Psalm 41:3)

And ye shall serve the Lord your God, and he shall bless thy bread, and thy water: and I will take sickness away from the midst of thee.

(Exodus 23:25)

And the Lord will take away from thee all sickness and will put none of the evil diseases of Egypt, which thou knowest, upon thee: but will lay them upon all them that hate thee.

(Deuteronomy 7:15)

Note: Relief in Time of Sickness

*M*any people are sick with various diseases such as diabetes, cancer, hypertension, sickle cell, etc. They are seeking relief in the medications and from home remedies; that someone may have told them about. Again, my friend Harriett was one that was diagnosed with Sickle Cell disease when she was age 5. She spent so much of her life in and out of the hospital. She didn't have much of a childhood because most of her friends would alienate themselves from her, because they feared that she would become ill while in their presence. She went from one doctor to another because of her illness.

As an adult she was told that she shouldn't bare children because of her disease, but she trusted God and He gave her that desire that she had in her heart to become to a Mother. Even though she wasn't living a life that was totally aligned with God,

She knew that prayer changed things. The scripture that God revealed to her was Matthew 19:26, "But Jesus said unto them, with men this is impossible, but with God all things are possible.

Even when the doctors tell you that there is nothing that they can do and it seems that there is no relief for your illness, pain, and/or suffering, know that God is in control of your situation and if you trust, believe, and have faith that he can and will do it, He can make what seems impossible, possible.

Let Us Pray

Bless the Lord, oh my soul and all that is within me bless his holy name for he has done great things. Heavenly father, we give you thanks for your grace and mercy toward us. We thank you, because you have been our keeper, our Provider, Protector, Deliverer, Miracle Worker, Waymaker and Healer. May your healing hand rest upon us, Holy Spirit touch every cell in our bodies with your healing power. Lord by your stripes we are healed from all sickness and diseases. In Jesus name. Amen.

COMFORT IN TIME OF SORROW

Unto the woman He said, I will greatly multiply thy sorrow and thy conception; in sorrow thou shall bring forth children; and thy desire shall be to thy husband and he shall rule over thee. (Genesis 3:16)

And He hath put a new song in my mouth, even praise unto our God: many shall see it, and fear and shall trust in the Lord. (Psalm 40: 3)

Yea, though I walk through the valley of the shadow of death. Will fear no evil: for thou art with me thy rod and thy staff they comfort me
(Psalm 23:4)

Comfort ye, comfort ye my people, saith your God. Behold, the Lord God will come with strong hand and His arm shall rule for Him; behold His reward is with Him and His work before Him. (Isaiah 40: 1-10)

Sing unto the Lord a new song, and His praise from the end of the earth, ye that go down to the sea and all that is therein; the Isles and the inhabitants thereof.
(Isaiah 42: 10)

Who comforteth us in all our tribulation that we may be able to comfort them which are in any trouble, by the comfort where with we ourselves are comforted of God.
(2 Corinthians 1:4)

Likewise the Spirit also helpeth our infirmities; for we know not what we should pray for as we ought: but the spirit also maketh intercession for us with groaning which cannot be uttered. (Romans 8: 26)

Blessed are they that mourn: for they shall be comforted. (Matthew 5:4)

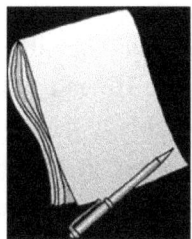

Note: *Comfort in Time of Sorrow*

*B*eing sorrowful can be related to death and sin. The bible tells us that "bl*essed are they that mourn for they shall be comforted.*" Matt. 5:4. After my mom passed away, I cried night and day, I did not attend her funeral because of the situation that I was in at the time of her death. A few years after my Dad passed away, it was also very hard for me, but God knew best, and he heard my cries. He sent the Holy Spirit to comfort me in my time of sorrow.

When people are going through sorrow as it relates to death, they often question God. They want to know how he could take away their loved one. They might even become angry with God because they feel that God is supposed to be a God of all good things. They are hurt and don't know who or what to turn to. John 14:18 says, "I will not leave you comfortless; I will come to you." If you allow God to comfort you through His word during your time of sorrow, you will understand that He is a God of love and things are done in His divine will.

If your sorrow is related to sin, the bible says, "to turn from your wicked ways and repent." Having a heart of repentance and turning away from those things that is so easy to get you off course will give you comfort in knowing that God loves you enough to forgive you and welcome you back into his loving arms.

Let Us Pray

Our father who art in heaven, Our heart is heavy with grief, Lord please send your holy spirit to comfort us and help us to comfort others who are grieving as your holy spirit have comforted us. We thank you for feeling our pain and sorrow. You word said as a mother comforts her child, so will you comfort us. Help us to sense your presence and your peace. Lord deliver us and, grant us peace within our hearts we pray. In Jesus name. Amen.

HOW TO CONTROL YOUR TONGUE

Keep thy tongue from evil and thy lips from speaking guile.
(Psalm 34: 13)

Concerning the works of men, by the words of thy lips I have kept me from the paths of the destroyer.
(Psalm 17:4)

A wholesome tongue is a tree of life; but perverseness therein is a breach in the spirit.
(Proverbs 15: 4)

Death and life are in the power of the tongue: and they that love it shall eat the fruit thereof.
(Proverbs 18:21)

If any man among you seems to be religious, and bridleth not his tongue, but deceiveth his own heart, this man's religion is vain. (James 1: 26)

And the tongue is a fire, a world of iniquity: so is the tongue among our members, that it defileth the whole body, and setteth on fire the course of nature; and it is set on fire of hell.
(James 3:6)

For he that will love life and see good day, let him refrain his tongue from evil and his lips that they may speak no guile.
(1 Peter 3: 10)

He that keepeth his mouth keepeth his life: but he that openeth wide his lips shall have destruction.
(Proverbs 13:3)

Speaking to yourselves in psalms and hymns and spiritual songs. Signing and making melody in your heart to the Lord: Giving thanks always for all things unto God and the Father in the name of our Lord Jesus Christ.
(Ephesians 5: 19-20)

By Him therefore let us offer the sacrifice of praise to God continually, that is, the fruit of our lips giving thanks to His Holy Name.
(Hebrews 13: 15)

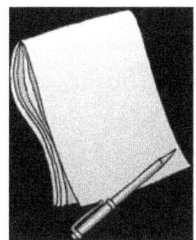

Note: How to Control your Tongue

*T*he power of life and death is in the tongue. Be careful what you speak over your life, and your children's life.

If you don't have good to say about someone, it is best you don't say anything. Stay positive! People who have unforgiveness, bitterness, hatred, and jealously in their heart, should let go and let God have His way in their lives. These people use their tongues unwisely. Be wise in how you use your tongue because you can cause things that are not of God to come upon your life. We should be wise and not foolish when we speak. The bible says, "We should be slow to speak". Please think before you say anything that could be harmful to you or anyone else.

Let Us Pray

Dear God, I commit to turn from idle words, foolishly talking and things that are contrary to my true desire for myself and towards others. Your words said there is the power of life and death in the tongue. I ask that you guide my tongue, when I want to criticize others. I am sorry for words I have spoken in anger or in gossip. Lord, please help me to realize when I am about to speak without thinking and to check my heart. Help me to be slow to speak. Help me to use my words to encourage, uplift, and wisely advise others. Help me Lord to be a person full of loving words, full of your sprit, overflowing with love, joy, peace, patience, kindness, gentleness and self-control. I choose your words for my lips; I choose your will for my life. Forgive me of my sins and lead me not into temptation. I pray that you will help me in this area in Jesus name I pray. Amen.

THERE IS POWER IN THE BLOOD

For the life of the flesh is in the blood: and I have given it to you upon the altar to make atonement for your souls: for it is the blood that maketh atonement for the soul.
(Leviticus 17:11)

For this is my blood of the new testament, which is shed for many for the remission of sins.
(Matthew 26:28)

But if we walk in the light, as he is in the light, we have fellowship one with another, and the blood of Jesus Christ his Son cleanseth us from all sin.
(1 John 1:7)

He that eateth my flesh, and drinketh my blood, dwelleth in me, and I in him.
(John 6: 56)

In whom we have redemption through his blood, the forgiveness of sins, according to the riches of his grace.
(Ephesian 1:7)

He shall redeem their soul from deceit and violence: and precious shall their blood be in his sight.
(Psalm 72:14)

Then answered all the people, and said, His blood be on us, and on our children.
(Matthew 27:25)

And being in an agony he prayed more earnestly: and his sweat was as it were great drops of blood falling down to the ground.
(Luke 22:44)

Whoso eateth my flesh, and drinketh my blood, hath eternal life; and I will raise him up at the last day.
(John 6: 54)

Much more then, being now justified by his blood, we shall be saved from wrath through him.
(Romans 5:9)

After the same manner also he took the cup, when he had supped, saying, this cup is the new testament in my blood: this do ye, as oft as ye drink it, in remembrance of me. For as often as ye eat this bread, and drink this cup, ye do shew the Lord's death till he come.
(1 Corinthians 11:25-26)

Let us pray

Most righteous God, our Refuge, our Deliverer, our Keeper and our strength; we give you glory; we honor you; we praise your holy name. Let your name be magnified and be lifted up above all other names, because you are our God, our savior and our king. Lord, cover us and our love ones under your blood. Build a fence all around us every day; Let no evil befall us according to psalm 91, nor let the enemy have dominion over us. Lord, remove us from darkness and bring us into your marvelous light. Guide our path, lead us so we will not kick our feet against a stone. Grant us uncommon favors and blessing; grant us healing and deliver us from the things that are a hindrance to our lives. Let your peace be with us and around us and let your blessings flow in everything we do and the lives we touch; and cause us to be a blessing to others. Cover us under your blood, pass your blood over our homes, church, children/grandchildren/family and friends. We give you thanks in Jesus name.
  Amen

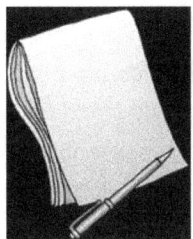

Note: *There is Power in the Blood*

*W*hen you are praying, ask the Lord to cover you and your family under His blood. Cover your home whenever you are leaving your home. There is power in the blood of Jesus. Through His blood, we are saved from our sin. His blood redeems us, there was a price against us that we could not pay, but the blood of Jesus redeemed us. There is fellowship in his blood, His blood brings us to fellowship with God. Without the blood of Christ, man is a long way from God. Peace in the blood, His blood reconciles our relationship with God. There is cleansing in his blood, His blood cleanse us from our sins. There is healing in his blood, there is no disease that His blood cannot cure. There is power in his blood over all evil forces. Did you know that when you say the blood of Jesus, that the devil and his imps have to back up? Halleluiah, There is power in the blood of Jesus!

When you are afraid in a time of mishaps, accidents, sickness or when someone is acting out of their character, all you have to do is plead the blood of Jesus or call upon the name of Jesus in that situation

Even when you are in situations of arguments, disagreements and/or disputes, you can plead the blood of Jesus over those situations as well. The devil is the author of confusion and the blood of Jesus can cause the devil to flee from the midst of those situations. When the enemy rise up against you on your job just plead the blood of Jesus. The blood will never lose its power!

The blood of Jesus is very powerful; it provides everything that we need to live a life of victory. Its washes away our sins. It gives us authority over the devil, there is healing, protection, deliverance, comfort, fellowship in the blood of Jesus. Thank you Lord.

HOW TO WAIT ON GOD

I waited patiently for the Lord; and he inclined unto me, and heard my cry. He brought me up also out of a horrible pit, out of the miry clay, and set my feet upon a rock, and established my goings. And he hath put a new song in my mouth, even praise unto our God: many shall see it, and fear, and shall trust in the Lord. (Psalms 40:1-3)

Wait on the Lord: be of good courage, and he shall strengthen thine heart: wait, I say, on the Lord.
(Psalm 27:14)

The Lord is good unto them that wait for him, to the soul that seeketh him. It is good that a man should both hope and quietly wait for the salvation of the Lord.
(Lamentations 3:25-26)

My soul, wait thou only upon God; for my expectation is from him. He only is my rock and my salvation: he is my defense; I shall not be moved.
(Psalm 62: 5-6)

They soon forget his works; they waited not for his counsel.
 (Psalm 106:13)

Let us hold fast the profession of our faith without wavering; (for he is faithful that promised.
 (Hebrews 10:23)

Therefore turn thou to thy God: keep mercy and judgment and wait on thy God continually.
(Hosea 12:6)

Therefore I will look unto the Lord; I will wait for the God of my salvation: my God will hear me.
(Micah 7:7)

Yea, let none that wait on thee be ashamed: let them be ashamed which transgress without cause. Shew me thy ways, O Lord; teach me thy paths. Lead me in thy truth, and teach me: for thou art the God of my salvation; on thee do I wait all the day. Let integrity and uprightness preserve me; for I wait on thee.
(Psalm 25:3-5- 21)

Note: How to Wait on God

Sometimes waiting is hard. We are a microwave generation and we want things done in the now. I am and have been waiting for God to save members in my family. I am not giving up because I know that God's timing and my timing are not the same.

Waiting on God is very important in our relationship with him and it also plays a key role in our spiritual development. Waiting on God for something can seems forever. But don't let it create bitterness or loss of hope. It can establish a deeper trust and knowledge of who God is and his everlasting love for us.

Continue to wait on God while praying and fasting about those areas of concern in your life. You will see the salvation of God if you continue to pray, fast, and wait on Him to do it.

Let us pray
Most Righteous and Eternal God, we give you glory and honor you Lord, because you alone are great. Father, today we give you thanks for one more day; a day that was not promised to us, a day to rest upon your words, which tell us, 'seek ye first the kingdom of God, and his righteousness; and all these things, shall be added unto you. 'According to Isaiah 40:33. They that wait upon the Lord shall renew their strength; they shall mount up with wings as eagles; they shall run and not be weary; and they shall walk, and not faint. Lord Teach me how to wait on you and not run before you. Without you I can't do anything. Because you gave me life, I pray that it's led by the Holy Spirit. A life that's in spirit and grace. Help me to be patient as I wait on you, because you have all power and wisdom and majesty and strength, you are the most high God. Help us to follow your example in Jesus name we pray

Amen

SIGN OF HIS COMING

Now the Spirit expressly says that in latter times some will depart from the faith, giving heed to deceiving spirits and doctrines of demons, speaking lies in hypocrisy, having their own conscience seared with a hot iron, forbidding to marry, and commanding to abstain from foods which God created to be received with thanksgiving by those who believe and know the truth.
(1 Timothy 4:1-3)

For the time will come when they will not endure sound doctrine, but according to their own desires, because they have itching ears, they will heap up for themselves teachers; and they will turn their ears away from the truth, and be turned aside to fables.
(2 Timothy 4:3-4)

And it shall come to pass in the last days, says God, that I will pour out of My Spirit on all flesh; Your sons and your daughters shall prophesy, Your young men shall see visions, your old men shall dream dreams .And on My servants and on my handmaidens I will pour out in those days of my Sprit; and they shall prophesy:(
Acts 2:17-18)

This know also that in the last days perilous times shall come. For men shall be lovers of their own selves, covetous, boasters, disobedient of parents, unfaithfulness, unholy.
2(Timothy 3:1-2)

The sun shall be turned into darkness, and the moon into blood, before that great and notable day of the Lord come: And it shall come to pass that whosoever shall call on the name of the Lord shall be saved,
(Acts 2:20 -21)

> Which also said, ye men of Galilee, why stand ye gazing up into heaven? This same Jesus, which is taken up from you into heaven, shall so come in like manner as ye have seen him go into heaven. (Acts 1:11)

For nation shall rise against kingdom: and there shall be famines, and pestilences, and earthquakes, in diver's places. All these are the beginning of sorrows. (Matthew 24:7 -8)

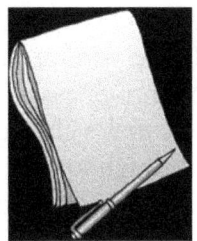

Note: *Sign of His Coming*

The Lord said in the last days we shall see signs and wonders, Nation against nation, you will hear of Wars and rumors of wars. Many will come in His name and say they are the Christ. There will be famines, pestilences and earthquakes in various places. All these things shall come to pass before the Lord appears. So, when you see wars and rumors of wars increasing do not pretend everything is normal, sit up and take notice! Jesus said that he will come again with power and glory. He will return not as child rather as a judge and king of the world. He said that he will come again on the clouds of heaven when celestial bodies and powers will be shaken. Jesus clarified that he will come at the end of the tribulation. He wants us to continue the preaching of His gospel to the entire world. He will come again to take the believers and to separate the sheep from the goats. In one of my visions the Lord showed me a disaster, It was so scary I began to cry, I said Lord what you want me to tell the people, he said tell the people to repent of their sin. Stay in the Word so you can know the truth and let no man deceive you. Jesus is coming soon. BE ready to meet your Savior.

Let us Pray

Father, we give you thanks for your saving grace and tender mercies towards us. We thank you for blessing us with another day, Lord we ask you for forgiveness of our sins and lead us not into temptation, Though we make choices and walk through the process of sanctification throughout our lives, all of our days are numbered, you are the God of our days and our lives. You heal the broken heart and ensure us that all will hear your words before Christ returns. Help us not to give up on others, because you will never give up on us, give us a heart like yours to love and forgive others that hurt us. Lord only you can change hearts, shift minds and enlighten souls to your truth. No one knows when you are coming but your father in heaven, until that day, protect all your people from all the evil forces of this world, from deceiving, lying and destroying your people, In Jesus mighty name. Amen.

www.ingramcontent.com/pod-product-compliance
Lightning Source LLC
LaVergne TN
LVHW091315080426
835510LV00007B/500